SCHIRMER PERFORMANCE EDITIONS

BEETHOVEN
PIANO SONATA IN C MAJOR
Opus 53 ("Waldstein")

T0082019

Edited and Recorded by Robert Taub

Also Available:
BEETHOVEN PIANO SONATAS
edited and recorded by Robert Taub

Volume I, Nos. 1–15
00296632 Book only
00296634 CDs only (5 disc set)

Volume II, Nos. 16–32
00296633 Book only
00296635 CDs only (5 disc set)

On the cover:
The Tree of Crows, 1822 (oil on canvas)
by Caspar David Friedrich
(1774–1840)
© Louvre, Paris, France/Giraudon/The Bridgeman Art Library

ISBN 978-1-4768-1630-2

G. SCHIRMER, Inc.

DISTRIBUTED BY
HAL•LEONARD®
CORPORATION
7777 W. BLUEMOUND RD. P.O. BOX 13819 MILWAUKEE, WI 53213

www.schirmer.com
www.halleonard.com

CONTENTS

BEETHOVEN
AND THE PIANO SONATAS

In 1816, Beethoven wrote to his friend and admirer Carl Czerny: "You must forgive a composer who would rather hear his work just as he had written it, however beautifully you played it otherwise." Having lost patience with Czerny's excessive interpolations in the piano part of a performance of Beethoven's *Quintet for Piano and Winds*, Op. 16, Beethoven also addressed the envelope sarcastically to "Herr von Zerni, celebrated virtuoso." On all levels, Beethoven meant what he wrote.

As a composer who bridged the gulf between court and private patronage on one hand (the world of Bach, Handel, Haydn, and Mozart) and on the other hand earning a living based substantially on sales of printed works and/or public performances (the world of Brahms), Beethoven was one of the first composers to become almost obsessively concerned with the accuracy of his published scores. He often bemoaned the seeming unending streams of mistakes. "Fehler—fehler!—Sie sind selbst ein einziger Fehler" ("Mistakes—mistakes!—You yourselves are a unique mistake") he wrote to the august publishing firm of Breitkopf und Härtel in 1811.

It is not surprising, therefore, that toward the end of his life Beethoven twice (1822 and again in 1825) begged his publishers C.F. Peters and Schott to bring out a comprehensive complete edition of his works over which Beethoven himself would have editorial control, and would thus be able to ensure accuracy in all dimensions—notes, pedaling and fingering, expressive notations (dynamics, slurs), and articulations, and even movement headings. This never happened.

Beethoven was also obsessive about his musical sketches that he kept with him throughout his mature life. Desk sketchbooks, pocket sketchbooks: thousands of pages reveal his innermost compositional musings, his labored processes of

creativity, the ideas that he abandoned, and the many others—often jumbled together—that he crafted through dint of extraordinary determination, single-minded purpose, and the inspiration of genius into works that endure all exigencies of time and place. In the autograph scores that Beethoven then sent on to publishers, further layers of the creative processes abound. But even these scores might not be the final word in a particular work; there are instances in which

Beethoven made textual changes, additions, or deletions by way of letters to publishers, corrections to proofs, and/or post-publication changes to first editions.

We can appreciate the unique qualities of the Beethoven piano sonatas on many different levels. Beethoven's own relationship with these works was fundamentally different from his relationship to his works of other genres. The early sonatas served as vehicles for the young Beethoven as both composer and pianist forging his path in Vienna, the musical capital of Europe at that time. Throughout his compositional lifetime, even when he no longer performed publicly as a pianist, Beethoven used his thirty-two piano sonatas as crucibles for all manner of musical ideas, many of which he later re-crafted—often in a distilled or more rarefied manner—in the sixteen string quartets and the nine symphonies.

The pianoforte was evolving at an enormous rate during the last years of the eighteenth century extending through the first several decades of the nineteenth. As a leading pianist and musical figure of his day, Beethoven was in the vanguard of this technological development. He was not content to confine his often explosive playing to the smaller sonorous capabilities of the instruments he had on hand; similarly, his compositions demanded more from the pianofortes of the day—greater depth of sonority, more subtle levels of keyboard finesse and control, and increased registral range.

These sonatas themselves pushed forward further development and technical innovation from the piano manufacturers.

Motivating many of the sonatas are elements of extraordinary—even revolutionary—musical experimentation extending into domains of form, harmonic development, use of the instrument, and demands placed upon the performer, the piano, and the audience. However, the evolution of these works is not a simple straight line.

I believe that the usual chronological groupings of "early," "middle," and "late" are too superficial for Beethoven's piano sonatas. Since he composed more piano sonatas than substantial works of any other single genre (except songs) and the period of composition of the piano sonatas extends virtually throughout Beethoven's entire creative life, I prefer chronological groupings derived from more specific biographical and stylistic considerations. I delve into greater depth on this and other aspects of the sonatas in my book *Playing the Beethoven Piano Sonatas* (Amadeus Press).

1795–1800: Sonatas Op. 2 no. 1, Op. 2 no. 2, Op. 2 no. 3, Op. 7, Op. 10 no. 1, Op. 10 no. 2, Op. 10 no. 3, Op. 13, Op. 14 no. 1, Op. 14 no. 2, Op. 22, Op. 49 no. 1, Op. 49 no. 2

1800–1802: Sonatas Op. 26, Op. 27 no. 1, Op. 27 no. 2, Op. 28, Op. 31 no. 1, Op. 31 no. 2, Op. 31 no. 3

1804: Sonatas Op. 53, Op. 54, Op. 57

1809: Sonatas Op. 78, Op. 79, Op. 81a

1816–1822: Sonatas Op. 90, Op. 101, Op. 106, Op. 109, Op. 110, Op. 111

From 1804 (post-Heiligenstadt) forward, there were no more multiple sonata opus numbers; each work was assigned its own opus. Beethoven no longer played in public, and his relationship with the sonatas changed subtly.

—*Robert Taub*

PERFORMANCE NOTES

Extracted from *Beethoven: Piano Sonatas Volume II*, edited by Robert Taub.

For the preparation of this edition, I have consulted autograph scores, first editions, and sketchbooks whenever possible. (Complete autograph scores of only twelve of the piano sonatas—plus the autograph of only the first movement of Sonata Op. 81a—have survived.) I have also read Beethoven's letters with particular attention to his many remarks concerning performances of his day and the lists of specific changes/corrections that he sent to publishers. We all know—as did Beethoven—that musical notation is imperfect, but it is the closest representation we have to the artistic ideal of a composer. We strive to represent that ideal as thoroughly and accurately as possible.

Tempo

My recordings of these sonatas are available as companions to the two published volumes. I have also included my suggestions for tempo (metronome markings) for each sonata, at the beginning of each movement.

Fingering

I have included Beethoven's own fingering suggestions. His fingerings—intended not only for himself (in earlier sonatas) but primarily for successive generations of pianists—often reveal intensely musical intentions in their shaping of musical contour and molding of the hands to create specific musical textures. I have added my own fingering suggestions, all of which are aimed at creating meaningful musical constructs. As a general guide, I believe in minimizing hand motions as much as possible, and therefore many of my fingering suggestions are based on the pianist's hands proceeding in a straight line as long as musically viable and physically practicable. I also believe that the pianist can develop senses of tactile feeling for specific musical patterns.

Pedaling

I have also included Beethoven's pedal markings in this edition. These indications are integral parts of the musical fabric. However, since most often no pedal indication is offered, whenever necessary one should use the right pedal—sparingly and subtly—to help achieve legato playing as well as to enhance sonorities.

Ornamentation

My suggestions regarding ornamental turns concern the notion of keeping the contour smooth while providing an expressive musical gesture with an increased sense of forward direction. The actual starting note of a turn depends on the specific context: if it is preceded by the same note (as in Sonata Op. 10 no. 2, second movement, m. 42), then I would suggest that the turn is four notes, starting on the upper neighbor: upper neighbor, main note, lower neighbor, main note.

Sonata in F Major, Opus 10 no. 2:
second movement, m. 42, r.h.

However, if the turn is preceded by another note (as in Sonata Op. 10 no. 2, first movement, m. 38), then the turn could be five notes in total, starting on the main note: main note, upper neighbor, main note, lower neighbor, main note.

Sonata in F Major, Opus 10 no. 2:
first movement, m. 38, r.h.

Whenever Beethoven included an afterbeat (Nachschlag) for a trill, I have included it as well. When he did not, I have not added any.

Footnotes

Footnotes within the musical score offer contextual explanations and alternatives based on earlier representations of the music (first editions, autograph scores) that Beethoven had seen and corrected. In areas where specific markings are visible only in the autograph score, I explain the reasons and context for my choices of musical representation. Other footnotes are intended to clarify ways of playing specific ornaments.

Notes on the Sonata[1]

PIANO SONATA NO. 21 IN C MAJOR, OPUS 53 ("Waldstein") (1803–04)

The expressive qualities of Sonata Op. 53 pushed to new heights the limit of what could be demanded from the piano. Virtuosity is demonstrated not exclusively through loud playing but rather by exquisite control: each movement of the "Waldstein" Sonata begins *pianissimo*, and among the most frequently used dynamic markings is *sempre pianissimo*.

Op. 53 is the first of the post-Heiligenstadt sonatas, and, along with his Symphony No. 3 ("Eroica"), immediately and palpably demonstrates Beethoven's extraordinary resolve to continue to develop his artistry. Both the "Eroica" Symphony and the "Waldstein" Sonata are strikingly original—even revolutionary. In both, the sonata form is expanded well beyond its previous conceptions.

The importance of the role of the first note, the bass C, cannot be overemphasized. I weight the left-hand chords slightly to the bottom, preserving the low C's all the way throughout mm. 1–2 and continuing the vector-like chromatic descent to the G octave in m. 11. This descent helps infuse the work with its unique tension and urgency. The first right-hand chord comes in very softly, almost secondary to the low C. Although the harmonic motion is striking, it actually proceeds quite slowly; therefore, I like a fast tempo—**Allegro con brio**, *pianissimo*—creating the feeling that the opening chords are pulsating restlessly.

The crescendo in mm. 21–22 continues all the way through to the *piano subito* in m. 23, setting up the arrival of B major dramatically. The B major harmony here must have a palpable presence; it cannot be too soft—it is marked only *p*, not *pp* as in the opening of the piece. Heard retrospectively as the dominant to E major, it helps establish the smooth transition to the second theme which is in the mediant key (E major), an unusual key relationship. In no previous sonata had Beethoven characterized the themes so strongly; the unexpected choice of key for the choralelike second theme enhances the overall contrast.

The marking for the second theme, *dolce e molto legato*, implies voicing the chords to the top (as initially indicated by the upper-voice stems). Both hands are legato, and changing fingering on several keys after playing them is frequently the only way to achieve a smooth, connected sound.

I consider this sonata to be in two movements, with the **Introduzione: Adagio molto** as a true introduction to the **Rondo: Allegretto moderato**. Unlike the Andante that Beethoven had originally intended as a second movement for this sonata, the Introduzione does not stand on its own musically; rather it is meant to prepare us expressively and emotionally for the Rondo that follows.

The pedalings designated by Beethoven at the opening of the Rondo, the very particular use of crossed hands, the *pianissimo*, the expansive harmonic rhythm, and the slightly raised dampers all make for extraordinary music. Removing any of these elements undermines the entire concept, a delicate and evanescent edifice that contributes mightily to the expressive revolution embodied within this work.

This Rondo is among Beethoven's most sophisticated, with sonata-like development and modulations, and careful and thorough markings. The two explosive middle episodes are in minor keys closely allied with the C major tonic—A minor (the relative minor) and C minor (the enharmonic minor). The leisurely pace suggested by the indication Allegretto moderato is in contrast to the driving pace of the first movement and the sense of inevitable forward motion generated by the descending chromatic bass—although slow—of the Introduzione. The brilliance of the Prestissimo coda, replete with octave glissandos and luminescent trills, is unprecedented.

I allow the tempo of the Prestissimo coda to be dictated by the speed required by the octave glissandos (m. 465); the tempo therefore is necessarily very fast. The harmonic motion here is actually quite slow, and we have heard the theme many times by this point in the piece. A very fast tempo to conclude the work is brilliant and rousing.

1 Excerpted from *Playing the Beethoven Piano Sonatas* by Robert Taub
edited and abridged by Susanne Sheston
© 2002 by Robert Taub
Published by Amadeus Press
Used by permission.

Dedicated to Prince von Waldstein

Sonata in C Major

Ludwig van Beethoven
Opus 53
Composed in 1803–04

Allegro con brio (♩ = 168)

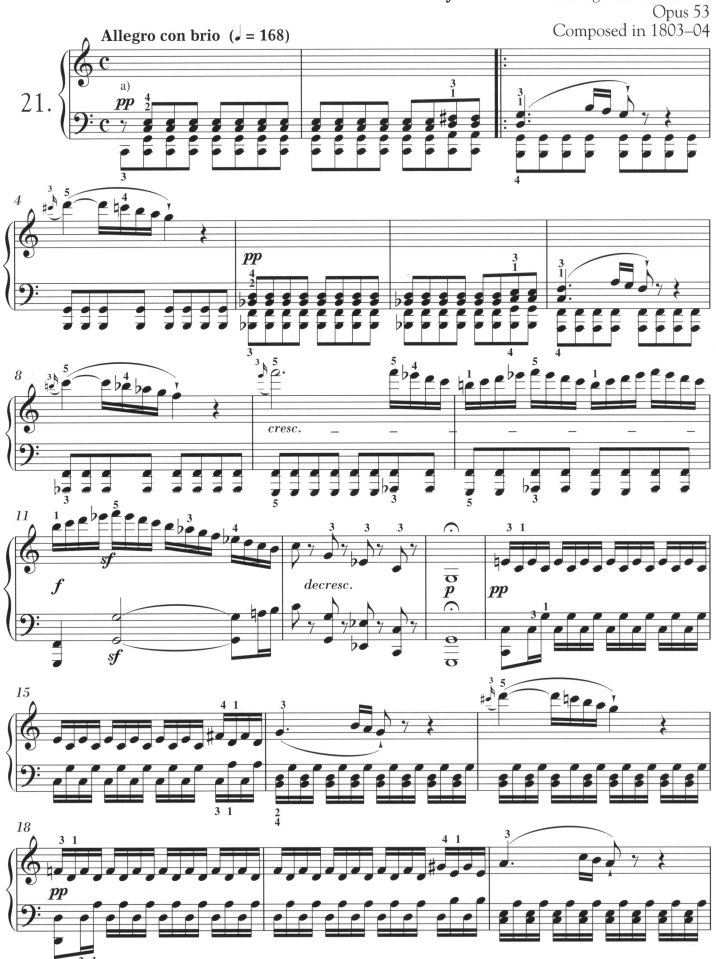

21.

a) The fingering in italics, and the pedal markings are Beethoven's.

b) An early proof of the first edition erroneously printed an F-flat here. In the first edition, one can observe the "ghost" of the " ♭," as it was smoothed out imperfectly from the copper engraving plate.

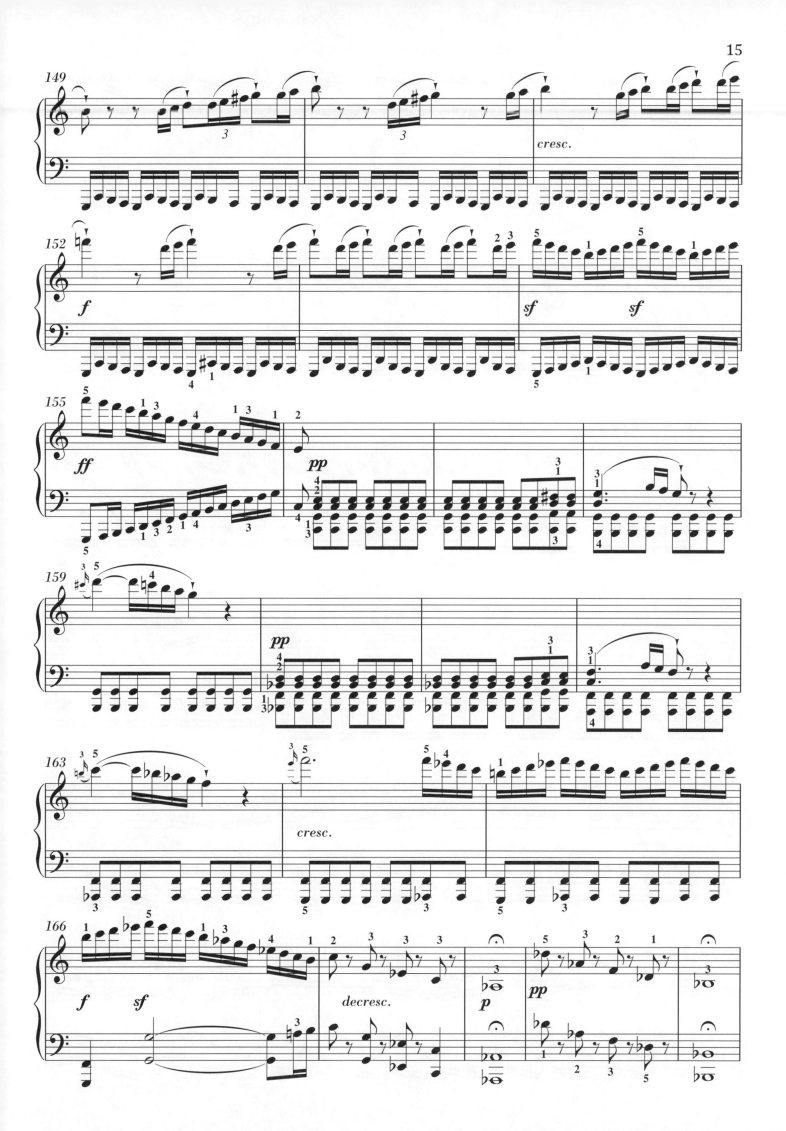

c) In the first edition B and D are engraver's errors.

INTRODUZIONE

Adagio molto (♪ = 50)

d) Thus in the first edition, perhaps through a misunderstanding; the better solution is since it is more important to emphasize the dissonance between C and D. In addition, the C continues a progression in the bass; the second B-flat does not.

RONDO
Allegretto moderato (♩ = 104)

Attacca subito il Rondo:

*sempre **pp***

e) Ped.

e) Beethoven's pedal markings create a delicate, diaphanous sonic mist. Contrary to common expectation, these pedal markings are challenging on both contemporaneous fortepianos and on modern instruments. However, the challenges are different. The pedal/damper technology on fortepianos is less precise than that of our modern grands, which in turn have greater sonorous capability. f) The motive starts with the low G. g) Some editions erroneously print a g^3 instead of f ^{3}.

24

h) First sixteenth note is detached to designate the beginning of the motive. i) Continue seamlessly the trill already in motion.

j) The last eighth rest denotes the release of the damper pedal.

Prestissimo ($\frac{1}{2}$ = 152)

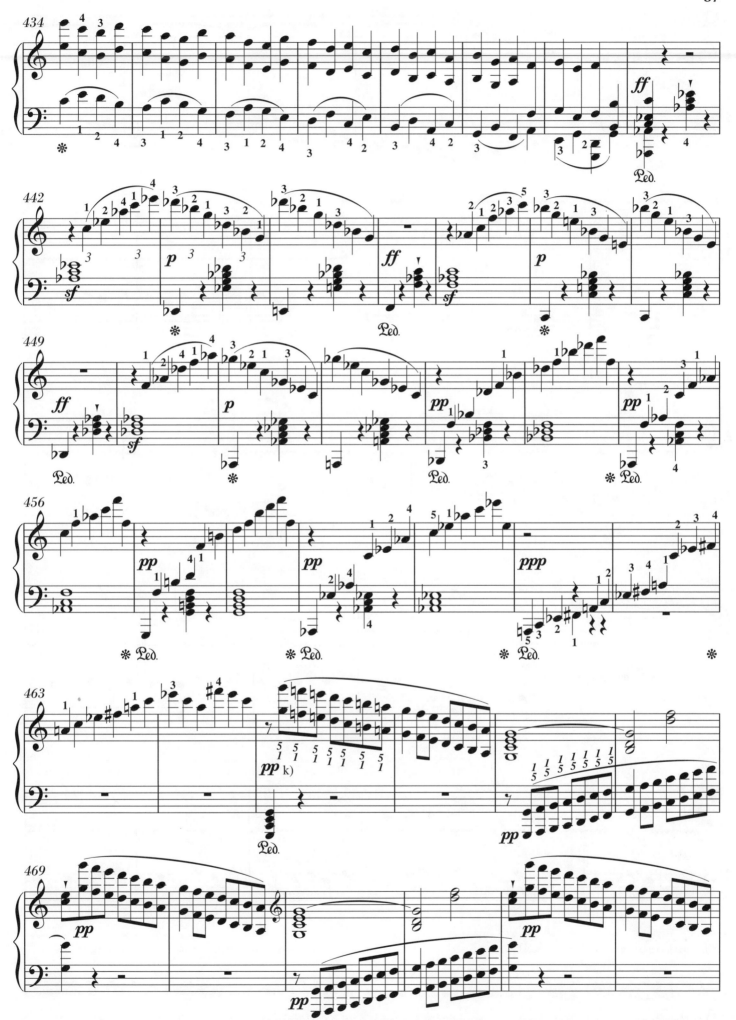

k) Beethoven's fingering, coupled with the fact that he provided no suggested simplification of this passage (as he did in the trills beginning in m. 485), implies that one hand plays an octave glissando; perfectly possible in—and consistent with—the context of this whirlwind Prestissimo Coda.

l) In the autograph manuscript, Beethoven noted: "Those for whom the trill, in combination with the theme, is too difficult, may simplify it the following way:

or if they are able to, may double it:

Two notes of each sextuplet are played to each quarter note in the bass. It doesn't matter if this trill loses some of its normal speed."

ABOUT THE EDITOR

Robert Taub

From New York's Carnegie Hall to Hong Kong's Cultural Centre to Germany's *avant garde* Zentrum für Kunst und Medientechnologie, Robert Taub is acclaimed internationally. He has performed as soloist with the MET Orchestra in Carnegie Hall, the Boston Symphony Orchestra, BBC Philharmonic, The Philadelphia Orchestra, San Francisco Symphony, Los Angeles Philharmonic, Montreal Symphony, Munich Philharmonic, Orchestra of St. Luke's, Hong Kong Philharmonic, Singapore Symphony, and others.

Robert Taub has performed solo recitals on the Great Performers Series at New York's Lincoln Center and other major series worldwide. He has been featured in international festivals, including the Saratoga Festival, the Lichfield Festival in England, San Francisco's Midsummer Mozart Festival, the Geneva International Summer Festival, among others.

Following the conclusion of his highly celebrated New York series of Beethoven Piano Sonatas, Taub completed a sold-out Beethoven cycle in London at Hampton Court Palace. His recordings of the complete Beethoven Piano Sonatas have been praised throughout the world for their insight, freshness, and emotional involvement. In addition to performing, Robert Taub is an eloquent spokesman for music, giving frequent engaging and informal lectures and pre-concert talks. His book on Beethoven—*Playing the Beethoven Piano Sonatas*—has been published internationally by Amadeus Press.

Taub was featured in a recent PBS television program—*Big Ideas*—that highlighted him playing and discussing Beethoven Piano Sonatas. Filmed during his time as Artist-in-Residence at the Institute for Advanced Study, this program has been broadcast throughout the US on PBS affiliates.

Robert Taub's performances are frequently broadcast on radio networks around the world, including the NPR (Performance Today), Ireland's RTE, and Hong Kong's RTHK. He has also recorded the Sonatas of Scriabin and works of Beethoven, Schumann, Liszt, and Babbitt for Harmonia Mundi, several of which have been selected as "critic's favorites" by *Gramophone*, *Newsweek*, *The New York Times*, *The Washington Post*, *Ovation*, and *Fanfare*.

Robert Taub is involved with contemporary music as well as the established literature, premiering piano concertos by Milton Babbitt (MET Orchestra, James Levine) and Mel Powell (Los Angeles Philharmonic), and making the first recordings of the Persichetti Piano Concerto (Philadelphia Orchestra, Charles Dutoit) and Sessions Piano Concerto. He has premiered six works of Milton Babbitt (solo piano, chamber music, Second Piano Concerto). Taub has also collaborated with several 21st-century composers, including Jonathan Dawe (USA), David Bessell (UK), and Ludger Brümmer (Germany) performing their works in America and Europe.

Taub is a Phi Beta Kappa graduate of Princeton where he was a University Scholar. As a Danforth Fellow he completed his doctoral degree at The Juilliard School where he received the highest award in piano. Taub has served as Artist-in-Residence at Harvard University, at UC Davis, as well as at the Institute for Advanced Study. He has led music forums at Oxford and Cambridge Universities and The Juilliard School. Taub has also been Visiting Professor at Princeton University and at Kingston University (UK).